Contents

Your child and numeracy

From September 1999, after a trial year in 1998, most primary schools must carry out a daily numeracy session, to meet new standards set by the government.

What is numeracy?

Numeracy is defined by the national Numeracy Task Force in the following way:

"Numeracy means knowing about numbers and number operations. More than this, it requires an ability and inclination to solve numerical problems, including those involving money or measures. It also demands familiarity with the ways in which numerical information is gathered by counting and measuring, and is presented in graphs, charts and tables."

Numeracy in the primary school

Numerate primary pupils are expected to:
• understand the size of a number and its position in the number system;
• know number facts by heart – times tables, bonds, doubles, halves;
• use these facts to work out answers mentally;
• calculate accurately in mental and written work, using a range of methods;
• know when they should or should not use a calculator;
• check and correct their own answers;
• explain their methods using mathematical vocabulary;
• measure and estimate sensibly;
• analyse data in tables, chart and graphs.

Numeracy teaching

The daily numeracy session will include whole-class, group and independent work and will incorporate as much mental and oral calculation as possible. Your child's teacher will be happy to explain the school's policy to you.

Turn to page 40 for ways to extend your child's numeracy skills.

How to use this book

As children progress through the Key Stage 1 years (ages 4–7), they acquire many reading, writing and mathematics skills which prepare for further education at Key Stage 2 and beyond.

Each book in this series is organised into 18 activity pages which provide practice in the skills your child will be developing at school.

Activities: Your child should use a pencil to fill in the activity pages. Take time to read any instructions together and to discuss the pictures.

Character: Gives tips, advice and key words.

Focus: The learning purpose of the page.

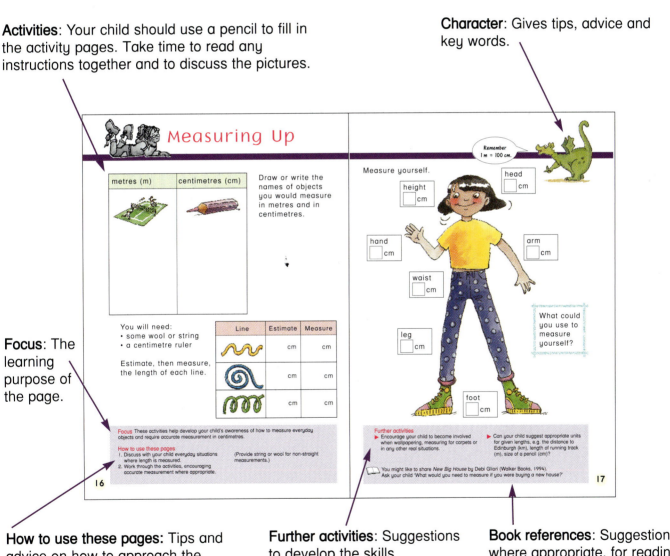

How to use these pages: Tips and advice on how to approach the activity.

Further activities: Suggestions to develop the skills highlighted on the page.

Book references: Suggestions, where appropriate, for reading books to help your child.

Remember, learning should be enjoyable. Work at your child's pace and emphasise successes rather than failures.

And finally, have fun!

Fairground

Andrew is at the fair. He catches these two ducks.

Add the scores.

 +  =

Add these scores.

7 + 3 =

1 + 9 =

3 + 8 =

7 + 5 =

4 + 7 =

Now try these.

2 + 5 + 7 =

3 + 2 + 4 =

6 + 3 + 6 =

9 + 1 + 7 =

8 + 1 + 2 =

Focus These activities develop your child's understanding of addition as the combination of more than one number (2 or 3) to make a total set

How to use these pages

1. Discuss the fairground scenario with your child, pointing out that Andrew and Jamilla are playing games in which they need to add up their scores.

2. Work through the problems together – allow your child to use counters if necessary, but also encourage rapid, mental recall of addition facts.

Jamilla must knock down 3 skittles. She needs to score 15 to win a teddy bear.

Jamilla scores 3 + 2 + 4 = ☐
What has she won?

What skittles must be knocked down to win these prizes?

Haunted House

11 children go into the haunted house.
3 children come out.
How many children are still inside?

11 − 3 = $\boxed{8}$

eleven − three = $\boxed{\text{eight}}$

There are now 8 children inside.
5 enter the hall of horrors.
How many are left now?

Write the sum in numbers.

☐ − ☐ = ☐

Now write it in words.

☐ − ☐ = ☐

Complete these sums.

13 − 5 = ☐   14 − 9 = ☐   15 − 7 = ☐   20 − 5 = ☐

18 − 6 = ☐   11 − 5 = ☐   12 − 10 = ☐   19 − 4 = ☐

Focus These activities will help to develop your child's understanding that subtracting a number makes another number less.

How to use these pages

1. Talk with your child about subtraction situations, e.g. when a friend leaves the classroom at school there are fewer children, or if he or she eats some sweets there will be fewer in the packet.

2. Collect words that mean 'take away' (minus, subtract, less).

3. Work through the problems, encouraging your child to use the door number line for counting back.

What other words mean 'take away'?

There are 9 ghosts. 4 fly away.
How many ghosts are left?

Use numbers ☐ – ☐ = ☐

Use words ☐ – ☐ = ☐

There were 11 spiders on the web.
Only 5 are left. How many crawled away?

11 – ☐ = 5   eleven – ☐ = five

Try these:

14 – ☐ = 6   13 – ☐ = 7

☐ – 3 = 7   10 – ☐ = 3

15 – ☐ = 8   ☐ – 6 = 5

6 – ☐ = 3   12 – ☐ = 8

☐ – 4 = 11   ☐ – 4 = 9

11 12 13 14 15 16 17 18 19 20

Further activities

▶ Encourage your child to respond rapidly to oral and written questions. Knowledge of subtraction facts to 10 will increase his or her speed and mental agility.

▶ Put subtraction into context, asking questions such as 'If there are 12 flowers in the garden and you pick 7, how many are left?'

Splish, Splosh!

Make a collection of bottles and containers. Label them A, B, C and so on. Sort them into three groups and write your results in the table.

less than I litre	about I litre	more than I litre

Now put the containers in order of size. Write them down in order here, with the smallest first.

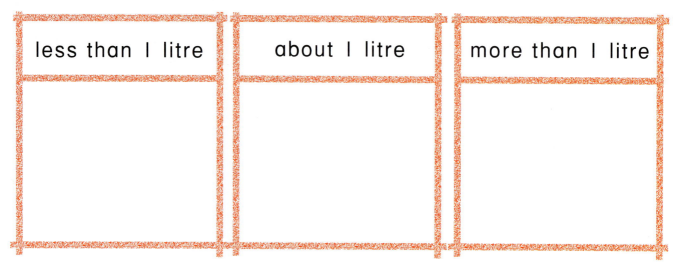

You will need three of your containers and a plastic cup.

How many cups does each container hold?

container			
estimated number of cups			
number of cups			

I have a **2 litre** tub of ice cream. After a week I have eaten half of it. How much is left?

Write the correct label under each picture.

| less than 1 litre | about 1 litre | more than 1 litre |

You have 50 litres of water in a barrel.
How many 10 litre buckets can you fill? _____

There are 4 children.
Each child drinks $\frac{1}{2}$ litre of lemonade. What size
bottle do you need to give them all a drink? _____

Mark's garden needs 25 litres of water.
How many times must he fill his 5 litre watering can? _____

9

How Many?

Look around the room.

In the table, write down the number of objects you can see of each colour.

colour	number of objects
blue	
black	
red	
green	
white	
yellow	

Now put the information on this bar chart.

10						
9						
8						
7						
6						
5						
4						
3						
2						
1						
0						
	blue	black	red	green	white	yellow

Focus These activities allow your child to collect, record, discuss and make predictions from numerical data using tables and bar charts.

How to use these pages

1. Work in a room that contains a range of different coloured objects. Can your child predict the most common colour?
2. Help your child to fill in the charts.
3. Have a packet of different coloured sweets for the second activity. Ask your child questions relating to the chart, such as 'How many more pink sweets than yellow are there?'

Which is the most popular colour? _____

Which is the least popular colour? _____

How many objects did you count altogether? _____

Would your bar chart look the same for a
different room? _____

Why? _____

Find a tube of sweets.
Empty them onto a plate.

Fill in the colours and make
a tally chart.

colour	tally

| = 1

|| = 2

||| = 3

|||| = 4

卌 = 5

Now draw a bar chart.

10
9
8
7
6
5
4
3
2
1
0

What colour are most sweets?

_____

What colour are fewest sweets?

_____

How many sweets are there
altogether? _____

Further activities

► There are limitless opportunities for collecting
and showing data. Your child could carry out
surveys for eye colour, birthday months,
favourite football teams, etc. It is always
important to follow this type of activity with
discussion about what the bar chart
shows.

► Can your child find bar charts in
newspapers, magazines, etc.? What
information is being shown?

Shape Names

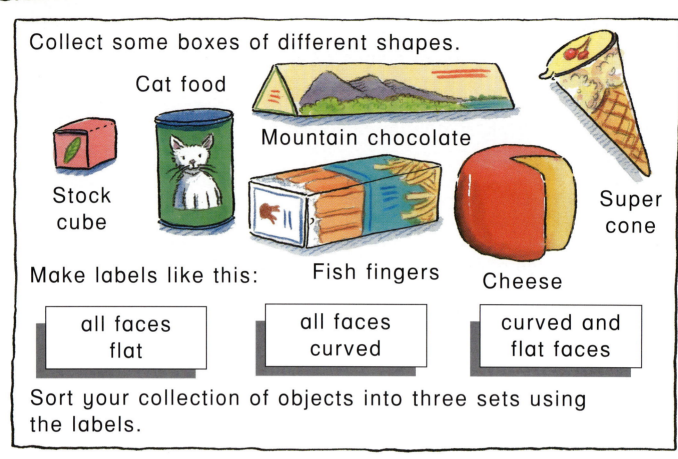

Collect some boxes of different shapes.

Cat food

Mountain chocolate

Stock cube

Fish fingers

Cheese

Super cone

Make labels like this:

| all faces flat |
| all faces curved |
| curved and flat faces |

Sort your collection of objects into three sets using the labels.

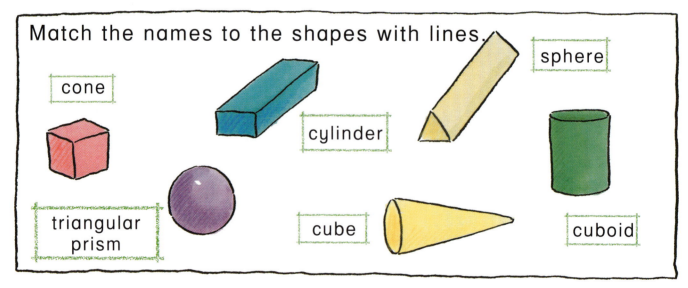

Match the names to the shapes with lines.

cone

sphere

cylinder

triangular prism

cube

cuboid

Focus These activities provide practice for your child in recognising 3-D shapes and sorting them according to different criteria.

How to use these pages

1. In advance, collect together an interesting selection of packaging and boxes.
2. Encourage your child to observe the differences between 2-D (flat) and 3-D (solid) shapes and to learn their names.
3. Ensure that your child understands the term 'face' (any flat side of a 3-D object) and 'edge', and then work through the activities.

What shape is your favourite cereal packet?

Fill in the table. Look back at the items on the opposite page to help you fill in the last column.

shape	how many corners?	how many edges?	name of the packet
sphere			
cylinder			
cube			
cuboid			
triangular prism			
cone			

Make these shapes from modelling clay. Cut them across the width.

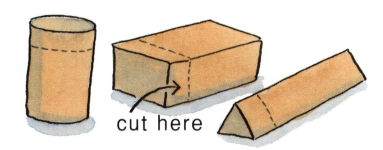

cut here

What do you notice? _____

Further activities

► Put the collection of 3-D shapes in a pillow case or other opaque bag. Your child can feel the shape and try to guess what it is, based on his or her knowledge of properties of 3-D shapes.

► Undo the boxes so your child can see the 'net', i.e. the flat shape that folds to make

the 3-D shape. Can your child make his or her own?

► Make two sets of cards, one with the names of 3-D shapes on, the other with a drawing of the shapes. Use these cards to play matching games.

Number Names

Match the words to the numbers.

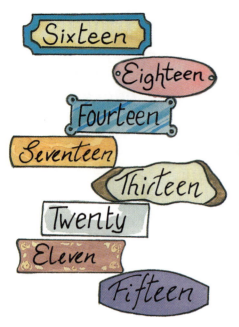

Sixteen
Eighteen
Fourteen
Seventeen
Thirteen
Twenty
Eleven
Fifteen

16	twelve
14	nineteen
19	sixteen
13	thirteen
20	eighteen
17	eleven
12	fifteen
18	seventeen
11	twenty
15	fourteen

You will need two dice.
Throw them and add the numbers.

Double this number and add 10.
Do this three times.

Write the answers in numbers and words.

_____   _____

_____   _____

_____   _____

Focus These activities offer your child practice in reading and writing numerals and number names, and in understanding ordinal numbers to denote position.

How to use these pages

1. Ask your child if they can remember any places where they have seen numbers. Are they sometimes shown as words?

2. Ensure your child is familiar with ordinal numbers (first, second, third). Help them to choose the correct ordinals to answer the questions.

Write the number names to 20 without looking! Were you right?

Answer these questions.

What is the seventh month of the year?_____

What is your first name? _____

What is the eighth letter of the alphabet? _____

Who is last on your class register? _____

Write the name of the second shape. _____

Write the name of the fourth shape._____

Write down these special numbers.

Can you think of any more?

your door number	your telephone number	your age	
people in your family	your favourite number	your date of birth	

Measuring Up

metres (m)	centimetres (cm)

Draw or write the names of objects you would measure in metres and in centimetres.

You will need:
• some wool or string
• a centimetre ruler

Estimate, then measure, the length of each line.

Line	Estimate	Measure
	cm	cm
	cm	cm
	cm	cm

Remember
1 m = 100 cm.

Measure yourself.

height
☐ cm

head
☐ cm

hand
☐ cm

arm
☐ cm

waist
☐ cm

leg
☐ cm

foot
☐ cm

What could you use to measure yourself?

Further activities
► Encourage your child to become involved when wallpapering, measuring for carpets or in any other real situations.

► Can your child suggest appropriate units for given lengths, e.g. the distance to Edinburgh (km), length of running track (m), size of a pencil (cm)?

 You might like to share *New Big House* by Debi Gliori (Walker Books, 1994). Ask your child 'What would you need to measure if you were buying a new house?'

17

Cut It Up

If you cut a sandwich into 2 equal pieces, each piece is a half ($\frac{1}{2}$).

Draw a line on each sandwich to show a different way of cutting the sandwich in half. Write $\frac{1}{2}$ on each half.

How many ways can you cut a sheet of paper in half?

_____

Do the halves have to be the same shape? _____

Now see how many ways you can cut the paper into 4 equal parts.

Each part is a quarter ($\frac{1}{4}$).

$\frac{1}{4}$	$\frac{1}{4}$
$\frac{1}{4}$	$\frac{1}{4}$

Focus These activities will help your child to recognise and use simple fractions in context.

How to use these pages

1. Provide your child with paper and scissors and let him or her explore the possibilities of making halves and quarters. Reiterate that the sections need to be the same size to be equal.

2. Work through the activities, reinforcing halves and quarters as being one of two and one of four equal parts respectively.

If I eat half a cake, how much do I have left?

Colour:

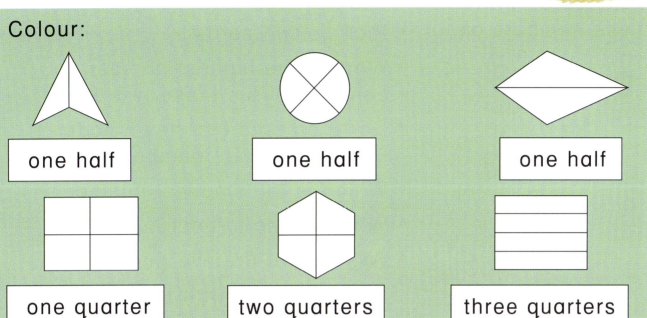

one half

one half

one half

one quarter

two quarters

three quarters

What fraction is shaded?

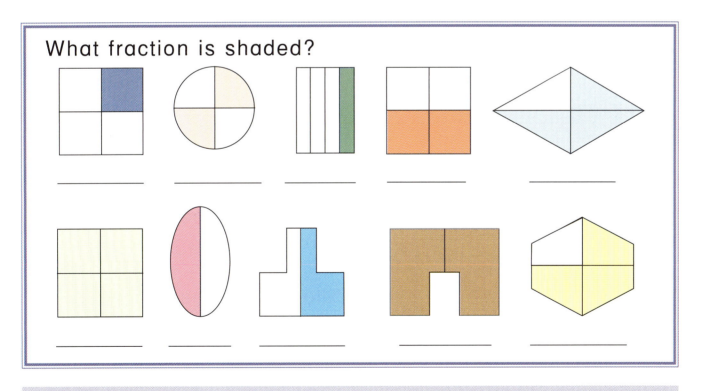

Further activities

▶ Provide your child with as many practical examples of fractions in context as possible, e.g. cutting cakes, pies, sandwiches, etc.

▶ Encourage your child to investigate how many ways there are of breaking up a bar of chocolate with squares, preparing your child for later fraction work.

 Share *A Piece of Cake* by Jill Murphy (Walker Books, 1991). Ask your child 'What fraction is the cake cut into?', 'In what different ways could you cut the cake?'

Hundreds of Numbers

Make cards with these numbers on.

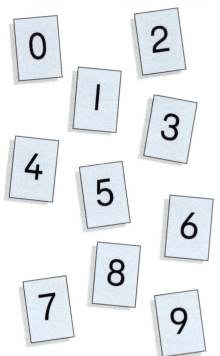

- Lay out the cards face down.
- Pick up two cards.
- What is the highest number you can make from those two cards? ☐
- Carry on until you have made 5 tens and units numbers.
- Which is the smallest number? ☐
- Which is the largest number? ☐
- Write down the five numbers in order, starting with the smallest.

☐ ☐ ☐ ☐ ☐

- Start again!

0	1	2	3	4	5	6	7	8	9
10	11	12							
20								28	
50					55				
						76			
80									
									99

Complete the 100 square.

Colour a number bigger than 17 but smaller than 40.

Colour a number smaller than 82 but bigger than 46.

Colour a number between 76 and 58.

Focus These activities develop your child's familiarity with numbers to 99 and emphasise the relevance and importance of each digit. These activities also aid understanding of the vocabulary of comparing and ordering numbers.

How to use these pages
1. Make a set of 0–9 numeral cards. The first activity can be repeated any number of times.

2. Work together on completing the 100 square before using it for the jigsaw activity. (Your child may need quite a lot of support to complete the 100 square.)

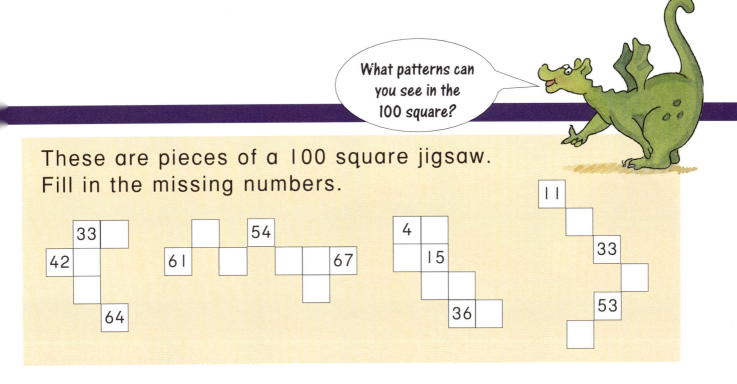

These are pieces of a 100 square jigsaw.
Fill in the missing numbers.

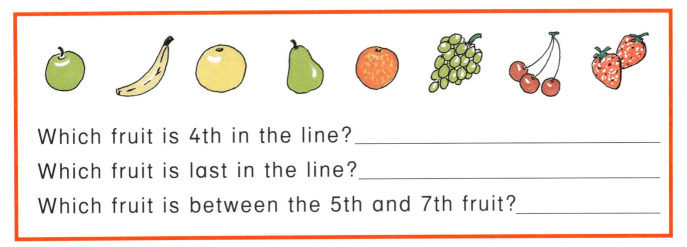

Which fruit is 4th in the line? _____

Which fruit is last in the line? _____

Which fruit is between the 5th and 7th fruit? _____

Anne   Jim   Zoë   Edie   Zak   Li   Reuben

Whose peg is 2nd? _____

Whose peg is 3rd from last? _____

Whose peg lies between Jim's and Edie's? _____

Further activities

▶ Use language associated with number and position when talking to your child about money, numbers of people, etc.

▶ Your child could make a 100 square and play 'Guess my number'. Pick a number and ask your child to guess it by asking estimating questions such as 'Is the tens number a 5? Is it odd? Does it end in a 3?' You can answer 'yes' or 'no'. Your child should colour the squares as they go to help eliminate the numbers.

Shape Pictures

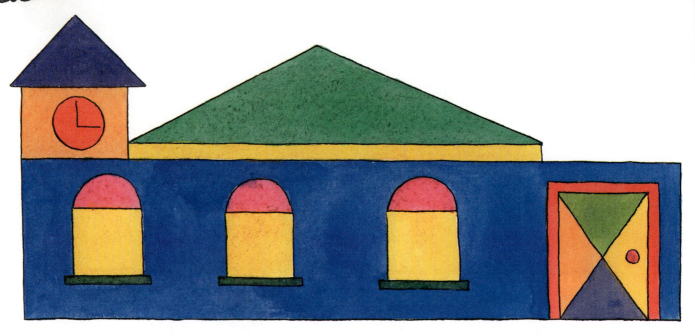

How many circles? ◯ _____   How many triangles? △ _____

How many squares? ▢ _____   How many rectangles? ▭ _____

How many semicircles? ◠ _____

Make a list of objects around you that are different shapes.

circles	rectangles	squares	triangles

Can you sort your objects in a different way?

Draw a dragon's face using as many different shapes as you can.

Find a scrap of paper.

Fold it in half.

Fold it in half again.

You now have a right angle (square corner) tester!
Use it to find the right angles in these shapes.
Colour each right angle like this:

Draw two shapes that have four right angles each.

. . . .

. . . .

. . . .

23

At the Post Office

Write down the value of each coin.

Jim is at the Post Office. Draw the coins he needs to pay for the stamp on this letter.

Jim has £1. How many 26p stamps can he buy for his postcards? _____

How much change will he get?

_____

Focus These activities will help your child to recognise the value of coins and solve problems involving money.

How to use these pages

1. Provide your child with some coins (the real thing is much better than plastic!) and match them with the pictures shown.

2. Discuss the Post Office scenario and all the services provided. Then support your child as he or she works through the activities, using a calculator where necessary.

When you go shopping, try to work out how much things cost and the change you get!

Jim buys:
- a ball of string for 35p
- a sheet of brown paper for 46p

Work out Jim's change from £1. _____
Draw the coins Jim could get in his change.

How much is this sheet of stamps worth? _____

Draw the coins Jim could use to pay for it.

A pack of envelopes costs 42p.

A pad of writing paper costs 23p more than a pack of envelopes.

How much is the pad of paper? _____

How much is a pad and a pack of envelopes together? _____

If Jim pays with six 20p coins, what change will he get? _____

Further activities

▶ Money activities are limitless and great fun! Setting up a shop, a post office, a café and providing 'real' situations will help your child to feel more confident when handling money and solving related problems.

 Talk about paying for stamps, sending letters, door numbers, etc. with your child as you share *The Jolly Postman* books by Janet and Allan Ahlberg (Heinemann, 1986).

Odd and Even

You will need 55 counters or buttons.
Lay them out like this.

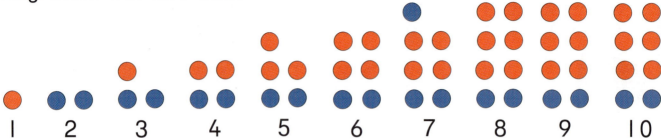

1 2 3 4 5 6 7 8 9 10

What do you notice?

_____

_____

For 2, 4, 6, 8 and 10 the counters are in sets of 2.
For 1, 3, 5, 7 and 9 there is one counter left over.

Numbers that make pairs are even.
Numbers that leave one extra are odd.

Colour the odd numbers red.
Colour the even numbers blue.

1	2	3	4	5	6	7	8	9	10
11	12	13	14	15	16	17	18	19	20
21	22	23	24	25	26	27	28	29	30
31	32	33	34	35	36	37	38	39	40
41	42	43	44	45	46	47	48	49	50

Can you see
a pattern?

Focus These activities aim to enable your child to recognise odd and even numbers.

How to use these pages

1. Provide your child with buttons or counters. Ask him or her to set them out as far as he or she can. Discuss how the odd numbers show an extra one each time.

2. Emphasise that odd and even numbers are recognisable by their last digit (units digit), i.e. 0, 2, 4, 6 or 8 in the units column means the number is even, whereas 1, 3, 5, 7 or 9 means odd.

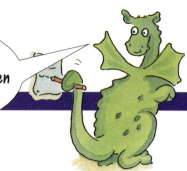

How old are you? Is it an odd or an even number?

All the yellow fish have odd numbers.
All the green fish have even numbers.

1 2 3 4 5 6 7 8 9 10

Add:

3 + 4 =

1 + 5 =

2 + 8 =

4 + 7 =

odd + even = _____

odd + odd = _____

even + even = _____

even + odd = _____

Do you think this is the same for all numbers?

Further activities

▶ Investigate small even numbers, using a calculator to divide by 2. Do the same for odd numbers. Discuss with your child what he or she notices – odd numbers will show x·5. Explain this as half a number and that it doesn't occur when dividing even numbers by 2.

▶ Encourage your child to count on in steps of 2 starting from an odd number or an even number, e.g. 7, 9, 11 or 10, 12, 14, 16. Again, does your child notice that the numbers continue to be odd or even, depending on the starting number?

27

Weighty Problems

Make a list of times when objects need to be weighed.

Decide which is the right weight. Tick ☑ the box.

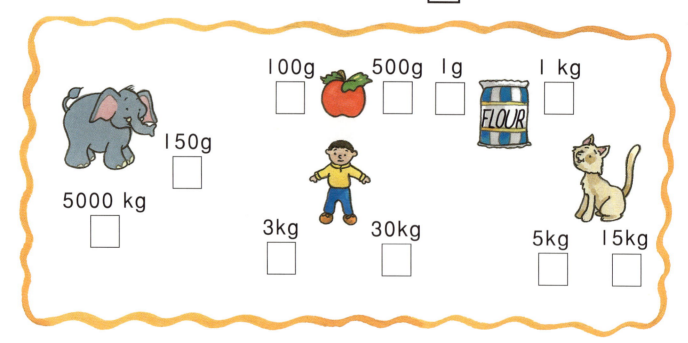

100g ☐   500g ☐   1g ☐   1 kg ☐

150g ☐

5000 kg ☐

3kg ☐   30kg ☐

5kg ☐   15kg ☐

Focus These activities promote awareness of the need for weighing, choosing suitable units to estimate, and using and interpreting scales.

How to use these pages

1. Discuss with your child occasions when babies, food, animals, etc. need weighing.
2. Encourage your child to distinguish between the lighter and heavier of two of the objects shown.
3. Follow the recipe together, allowing your child to use kitchen scales and encouraging accuracy.
4. Help your child to read the scales shown.

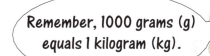
Remember, 1000 grams (g) equals 1 kilogram (kg).

Cherry Cakes

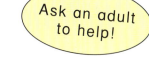
Ask an adult to help!

Ingredients:
50g self raising flour
50g sugar
50g margarine
25g glacé cherries (chopped)
1 egg

What to do:
1. Ask an adult to set the oven to 200°C/Gas Mark 5.
2. Weigh out the ingredients and put eight cake cases in a bun tray.
3. Place all the dry ingredients in a bowl, except the cherries.
4. Beat the egg and add to the dry ingredients.
5. Beat for two minutes with a wooden spoon (or one minute with an electric whisk).
6. Add the chopped cherries and divide the mixture equally between the cake cases.
7. Ask an adult to place in the oven for 10–15 minutes until golden.

Write the weights.

☐ g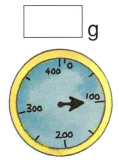

☐ g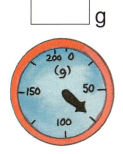

☐ g

Further activities
▶ Any simple recipe can be followed in order to gain practice in reading scales.
▶ Encourage your child to estimate the weight of objects when out shopping.

▶ Make a collection of sets of objects of a similar weight, and place them in plastic bags. Ask your child to guess the weights. Using scales, weigh them and see how accurate your child's estimates were.

Multiplication Menu

There are 6 eggs in a box.

How many eggs in 3 boxes?

6 x 3 = ☐

How many eggs in 5 boxes?   ☐ x ☐ = ☐
How many eggs in 10 boxes?   ☐ x ☐ = ☐

There are 8 tomatoes in a pack.

How many tomatoes in 5 packs?   ☐ x ☐ = ☐
How many tomatoes in 10 packs?   ☐ x ☐ = ☐

Focus These activities will help develop your child's understanding of multiplication as repeated addition.

How to use these pages

1. Ask your child to think of situations when you have been shopping and you have had to multiply in order to get the right number of items.

2. Work through the activities, encouraging the use of counters laid out in sets if your child is unsure of his or her multiplication facts.

Remember x means 'times' or 'lots of' or 'multiply by'.

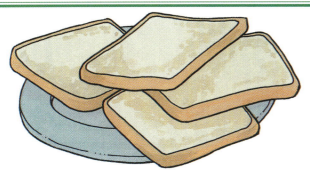

There are 8 slices of bread in a packet.

How many slices in 2 packets? ☐ x ☐ = ☐

How many slices in 5 packets? ☐ x ☐ = ☐

Here is a menu for breakfast in a hotel.

Breakfast

1 egg
2 slices of bread
1 tomato

Write a shopping list to buy enough food for 24 people's breakfasts.

—— boxes of eggs
—— packs of tomatoes
—— loaves of bread

Try these:

2 x 5 = ☐

3 x 4 = ☐

6 x 2 = ☐

7 x 5 = ☐

10 x 5 = ☐

3 x 3 = ☐

☐ x 2 = 8

☐ x 5 = 10

3 x ☐ = 3

Further activities

▶ Ask your child to imagine he or she is having a party. How many people will be invited? Decide on food that comes in packets, e.g. boxes of cakes, bags of crisps, cartons of drinks. Using multiplication facts decide how many of each you would need to buy for the party.

▶ Ask your child to throw 2 dice. Can he or she multiply the two numbers? Do they get any of the same answers from multiplying different numbers together on the dice?

31

Share It Out

Choose one of these numbers.

8 **12** **20** **18** **6** **2** **14**

10

Count out that number of counters.

Share out the counters between you and your helper.

For example
if you picked
6 ÷ 2 = ☐

Six shared equally between two is three.

Six divided by two equals three.

	divided by 2	is
6	⟶	_____
2	⟶	_____
14	⟶	_____
10	⟶	_____
8	⟶	_____
12	⟶	_____
18	⟶	_____
20	⟶	_____

Fill in the chart.
Do this for all
the numbers.

Try planting some sunflowers yourself. How tall do you think they might grow?

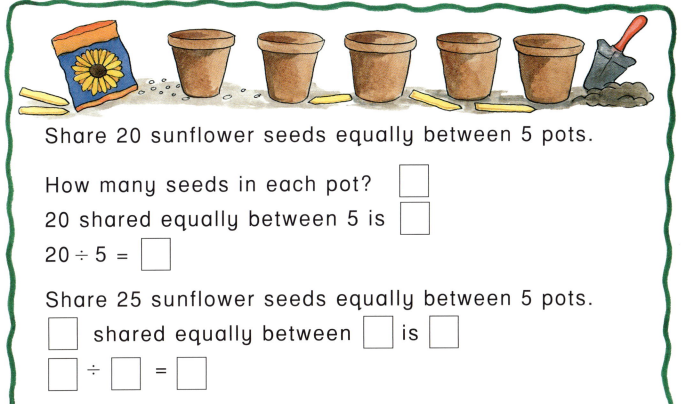

Share 20 sunflower seeds equally between 5 pots.

How many seeds in each pot? ☐

20 shared equally between 5 is ☐

20 ÷ 5 = ☐

Share 25 sunflower seeds equally between 5 pots.

☐ shared equally between ☐ is ☐

☐ ÷ ☐ = ☐

Answer these:

8 sweets between 4 children is 8 ÷ 4 = ☐

10 pencils between 5 pots is ☐ ÷ ☐ = ☐

15 sandwiches between 3 plates is ☐ ÷ ☐ = ☐

20 straws between 10 cups is ☐ ÷ ☐ = ☐

18 tables between 2 classrooms is ☐ ÷ ☐ = ☐

Further activities

► Ask your child to plan a picnic menu for the family. All items of food need to be shared equally among the number of people (avoid using remainders).

► Change the number of people. Will that affect how the food is shared out? The sharing operations could be recorded using the ÷ sign.

 Share *The Lighthouse Keeper's Picnic* by Ronda and David Armitage (André Deutsch, 1993). Ask your child to design a picnic for a lighthouse keeper, asking 'How much food is needed?', 'How will it be shared out?'

Jumping Jack

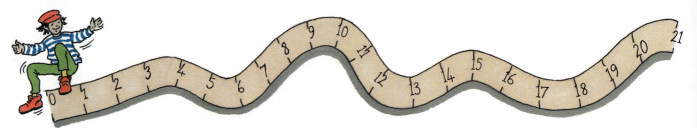

Jumping Jack starts on 0.

How many jumps of 2 are needed to reach 12? ☐

How many 2s in 12? ☐ $12 \div 2 =$ ☐

How many jumps of 2 are needed to reach 18? ☐

How many 2s in 18? ☐ $18 \div 2 =$ ☐

How many jumps of 3 are needed to reach 15? ☐

How many 3s in 15? ☐ $15 \div 3 =$ ☐

How many jumps of 3 are needed to reach 21? ☐

How many 3s in 21? ☐ $21 \div 3 =$ ☐

---

12 pencils.

Ring groups of 3.

12 pencils in groups of 3.

There are ☐ groups.

$12 \div 3 =$ ☐

Focus These activities will help your child to understand the operation of division as grouping.

How to use these pages

1. Encourage your child to see division as grouping, i.e. $18 \div 3$ means 'how many groups of 3 can be made from 18?' rather than 'sharing 18 equally among 3'.

2. Work through the activities, encouraging your child to ring/colour/cross off the groups to help him or her solve the problems.

Use Jumping Jack's number line to help you.

16 stickers.

Each child can have 2 stickers.

How many children can have stickers? 16 ÷ 2 = ☐

☐ children can have stickers.

15 flowers.

Each vase needs 3 flowers.

How many vases can be filled? ☐

☐ ÷ ☐ = ☐

Try these.

12 ÷ 2 = ☐   10 ÷ 2 = ☐   8 ÷ 2 = ☐

14 ÷ 2 = ☐   4 ÷ 2 = ☐   20 ÷ 2 = ☐

 9 ÷ 3 = ☐   16 ÷ 2 = ☐   15 ÷ 3 = ☐

18 ÷ 3 = ☐   12 ÷ 3 = ☐   18 ÷ 2 = ☐

Further activities

▶ Encourage your child to see division as the reverse of multiplication, so that 14 ÷ 2 is 'how many 2s make 14?'. Knowledge of multiplication facts is very important in aiding accuracy and speed of response.

▶ Devise multiplication quizzes and make matching division/multiplication cards, e.g. 12 ÷ 4 = 3 matches 4 x 3 = 12.

▶ Set out a number of counters as an array, e.g. 12 as 4 rows of 3. Write two multiplication facts and two division facts for each array, i.e. 4 x 3, 3 x 4, 12 ÷ 3, 12 ÷ 4, encouraging visualisation of number facts.

What Time is it?

				JULY		
Monday	Tuesday	Wednesday	Thursday	Friday	Saturday	Sunday
				1	2	3
4	5	6	7	8	9	10 *Sarah's party 6 p.m.*
11	12 *Dentist 3.45 p.m.*	13	14	15	16	17
18	19	20	21	22 *Break up for holidays!*	23	24
25	26	27 *Take Bailey to vet 1.15 p.m.*	28	29	30	31

How many days are there in July? _____

On what day of the week is July 9th? _____

How many Thursdays are there in July? _____

When do the summer holidays begin? _____

How many days are there in one week? _____

Show the time of the dentist's appointment.

Show the time of Bailey's vet appointment.

If the vet appointment lasts for half an hour, show the time it will finish on both clocks.

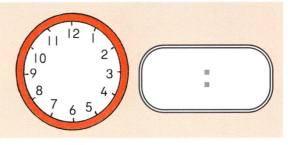

What can you do....?

in 10 seconds	in 1 minute	in 1 hour

Further activities

▶ Using a TV guide, ask your child to work out how long his or her favourite shows last, and to plan an evening's viewing.

▶ Estimate the time it takes to walk to the shops, etc. Then measure the time on either a digital or analogue clock.

 Use the following books to discuss a range of time-related topics: *The Very Hungry Caterpillar* by Eric Carle (Puffin, 1974) for the days of the week; *The Bad Tempered Ladybird* by Eric Carle (Hamish Hamilton, 1978) for reading time; *Five Minutes Peace* by Jill Murphy (Walker Books, 1988) for sequencing events in time.

Number Fun

You need three dice.

die 1	die 2	die 3
5	5	3

Show all the ways you can score 13 in the table.

How many ways can you find of scoring 15?

die 1	die 2	die 3
5	5	3

You need a set of dominoes.

Draw the dominoes whose dots have an odd total.

How many dominoes have a total of 7 dots? ☐

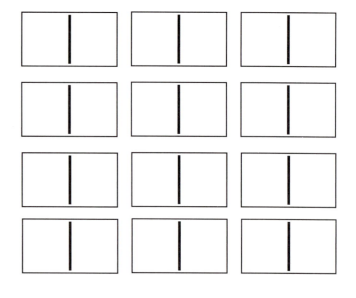

Make up your own number game using playing cards.

Write down seven questions which have the answer 10.
Use +, −, x and ÷ .

[ ]

[ ]

[ ]

[ ]

2 x 5

[ ]

[ ]

[ ]

Look at the magic square.

4	3	8
9	5	1
2	7	6

Add the numbers in:
• each column
• each row
• across the diagonals.

Why is it a magic square?

		7
4	6	8
5		

Fill in the missing numbers in these magic squares.

4		6
9		
8		10

Further activities

▶ Make some cards showing digits (0–9) and the operational signs (x, −, +, ÷ and =). Give your child say, 3 digits, 2 signs and the equals card. See how many different sums and answers he or she can make. Then swap one of the digits and ask 'What can you make now?'

▶ Change the octopus number and challenge your child to find eight questions in a limited time. Try to reduce the time allowed each time the activity is repeated – just for fun!

39

Helping your child

Develop your child's mathematics skills

Learning about maths is not just about learning numbers. It is about developing an awareness of numbers in the environment – numbers in the street, at home, in the shops.

There are many ways to help your child develop his or her numeracy skills.

- Estimate and weigh fruit and vegetables in the supermarket. Guess quantities and perform mental calculations. Identify the coins that will be needed to buy items in the shop or work out the amount of change.

- Count the number of objects in the trolley and name the shapes of different packaging. Sort the packets according to different criteria.

- At home, lay the table, matching items in each setting and counting items. Encourage your child to help measure out ingredients, cut halves and quarters and work out cooking times. Place different containers in order of capacity.

- Read analogue and digital clocks and relate the times to real events. Look again later and work out periods of time that have elapsed. Identify start and finish times of television programmes.

- Plant out bulbs and seeds in pots, counting as you do so. Use a calendar to work out when plants will flower.

- Look at different numbers used around the home, e.g. door numbers, telephone numbers and dates. Encourage your child to say the numbers aloud.

- Sort toys according to type, size, shape etc. Set up a play shop, post office or restaurant using real money and objects. Construct shapes from modelling kits, Plasticine or junk. Encourage your child to use shape and positional language.

- Ask questions that require mental calculations such as: you have got 8 pencils, how many more do you need to have 12? Play board games using counters and dice.

- Ask questions such as 'How many circles can we count on our journey?' Count objects and perform mental calculations.

- Compare sizes of objects, and match objects that are the same. Make collections of nature objects, such as leaves or twigs, and arrange them in sets of similar weight.

Take It Away: Subtraction Problems

20 19 18 17 16 15 14 13 12 11 10 9 8 7 6 5 4 3 2 1

□ = □ = □ = □ =
— — — —
□ □ □ □

□ = □ = □ = □ =
— — — —
□ □ □ □

□ = □ = □ = □ =
— — — —
□ □ □ □

Picnic Time: Data Handling

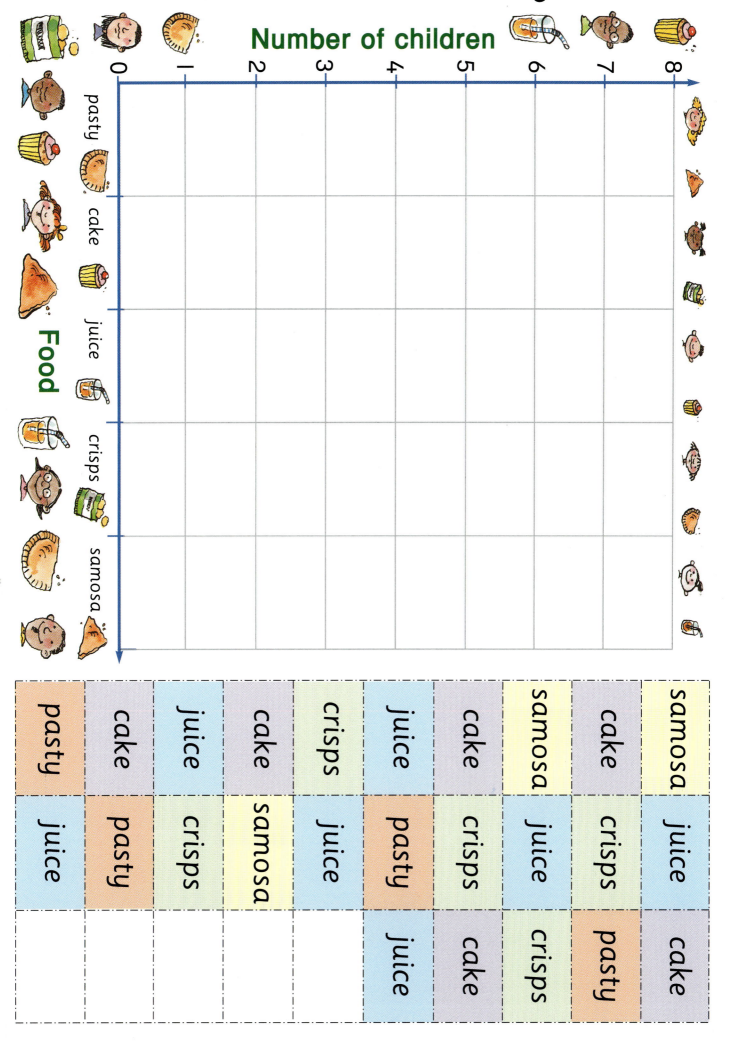

100 Number Square

1	2	3	4	5	6	7	8	9	10
11	12		14	15	16		18	19	20
21	22	23		25		27	28		30
	32	33	34		36	37		39	40
41		43	44	45	46		48	49	
51	52		54	55		57	58		60
61	62	63		65	66	67		69	70
	72	73	74		76		78	79	80
81		83	84	85		87	88		90
91	92		94	95	96	97		99	100

Colour the squares:

Ending in 1 green
Ending in 2 red
Ending in 3 yellow
Ending in 4 blue
Ending in 5 purple
Ending in 6 orange
Ending in 7 light green
Ending in 8 pink
Ending in 9 grey
Ending in 10 brown

Cut-out number cards:

56	35	82
31	68	50	26
93	17	47	59
38	71	86	29
77	89	13	42
24	98	53	64

Calendar Clock

The date today is

Monday	Tuesday	Wednesday	Thursday	Friday	Saturday	Sunday
January	February	March	April	May	June	
July	August	September	October	November	December	

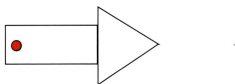
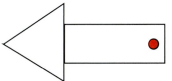